What is
God is Love

*One Woman's Journey
from Growing up in Care,
Escaping from Sex Work
and Rebuilding her Life.*

By Kim Chaulk

Contents

Introduction

This frank account exists because I want people to know how what happened to me in childhood led me into the life I led as a sex worker until 1991. It also shows that, although history can seem to repeat itself through the generations, through being born again I found the courage and inspiration to break the cycle and change the way I live my life.

I talked into a recorder for several hours and my account was edited into the following story. It is written in my own words as much as possible. Names and places have not been changed.

My Childhood

When I was born in 1957, my mother Kitty was only 17, and had been abandoned by her boyfriend. He was an American serviceman based at Upper Heyford in Oxfordshire, who went off back to America. Kitty was heartbroken and could not cope with her baby so she gave me to her parents to bring up, even though her mother had serious epilepsy and her father was a drinker and a gambler. Sometimes he lost so much that there was no money left even for food, and I went hungry.

Like many people, I do not remember much detail from my childhood, but more a series of snapshots. I feel that sometimes the brain just blocks out things is can't comprehend. What I do remember are the feelings that arose from what happened to me, particularly the feeling of not being loved and cared for.

My grandfather was sterna and stiff. He was very strict and I'll never forget one time when I was very young, he came up to bring me something to eat, and he pulled the blankets off me. That was when he'd come back from the pub, or something like that. He wanted to talk, even though it was the middle of the night, something like 12 o'clock or 1 o'clock, and I needed my rest for going to school. The problem was that I slept at school – I really didn't get much education at all because I was always falling asleep in class.

I often witnessed my grandmother's epileptic fits and recognised the signs when they were coming on. I would desperately try to get my grandma to jolt her way out of it. I would say "Mum! Mum!" (which is what I called her because that was how I thought of her). "Wake up, wake up!" But I was never successful, and was left feeling helpless and somehow responsible. I couldn't always be at home, and I felt my grandmother should never be in the house on her own at all.

I remember when I was about 8 years old, my grandmother had a fit and her hand went in the fire, and I didn't know what to do. I called the neighbour next door and she came and helped. She went into Littlemore (WHAT IS THIS?) because of her epilepsy.

I would often go out on my bike and ride around all day on my own until dusk fell because there was no life at home, no loving, no kindness. I felt lonely and unloved. Although I was being fed and clothed my grandparents were clearly unable to provide the loving nurture that children need.

One of the most remarkable aspects of my story is that I am still in touch with the social worker, Deirdre, who took my case when I first came to the attention of Social Services in 1969. Deirdre recalls that she first met me at my school in Marsh Lane, Oxford, and remembers that I spent quite a lot of time with my domestic science teacher who seemed to have taken me under her wing. I remember that this teacher lived in Sandford, although I never visited her at her home. My memory is that my aunty Pat (my birth mother's sister) was so concerned about me that she contacted Social Services when I was about 11, and I was taken into care. Deirdre was allocated my case and remembers her first visit to my home, how dark and dreary my home was, and my grandparents were too.

Me and my friend had been hitching lifts with lorry drivers. As Deirdre and her colleagues could not stop us from doing this, it was decided that I should go to live in Windmill House, a children's home in Windmill Road Oxford.

I found that to be a good place to be and I liked the other youngsters. The boys were upstairs and the girls were downstairs. The carers were just ordinary people. I liked some of them but others were very stern, especially the male one. I remember being punished for some transgression – I'm not even sure what it was – and he made me stand in one of the cloakrooms on a cold floor for over an hour. It was horrible and I've never forgotten it.

When I was about 12, my birth mother Kitty (who by now had married an American) came back to Oxford with her husband and two children. She tried to get me out of Windmill House to see whether I could cope and fit in with my new family. Deirdre says that she and her colleagues did not want me to go and stay with them right away, but wanted me to get to know them more slowly.

However she says that I was quite naturally desperate to join my family as soon as possible, but having done so, I found it quite difficult. This was because there were now two half sisters and my stepfather was very strict. He turned out to be an alcoholic who took to beating me. Often, I didn't know why. I think it may have been something I said, or that I had shouted at him. I wanted to do things my way, but he didn't like that, so he got his belt out and beat me. My mother didn't stop him. I stuck it out for two months but it didn't work out and I went back to the children's home. Kitty and her husband went back to the States and had two more children.

I didn't see them again for over 20 years. My mother didn't keep in contact and I often wondered where she was. It hurt that the links seemed to have been severed. After all, I was her first born and she must have wondered how I was getting on. This experience added to my feelings of being unwanted and rejected. Aunty Pat stayed in touch, but only occasionally when she came and saw her mum and dad with her children. My other aunt Kay, lived in Australia.

Growing up in Care

Eventually, when I was about 13, I was transferred to Upper Heyford Remand Home because I kept on absconding back to my grandparents' home which was in Slade, in Oxford, not far from Windmill House. I felt that that was where I had grown up and where I should be and it wasn't far to run. I didn't understand why I was living in a children's home and felt I hadn't done anything wrong. I just kept on returning "home" and Deirdre says that's why they decided to lock me up in a remand home. I found the Upper Heyford home really strange. Nobody talked much and everyone kept to themselves. There was a teacher there who drew charcoal portraits. I was given mine and I have kept it ever since:

Charcoal Portrait of me in 1972 at aged 14

Then eventually, when I was about 14, they sent me to another secure home called Monmouth House. Being so far away from Oxford, it was felt that I would be less likely or able to run away.

Monmouth House was a horrible place. It was like a nunnery, and the girls there were harming themselves. They were swallowing nails, cutting themselves – everything. It was dreadful. If any of the girls did something wrong, we were put in the basement and would be made to stay there for hours. The girls had to do all the cleaning – and I hated polishing. We had to attend school, but we didn't learn much apart from machine sewing, how to make dresses and typing. It was just the basics.

All this reinforced my feelings of insignificance, and there were times when I felt nothing but abandoned by my mum and rejected by my grandparents.

Eventually, me and my friend – we were about 15 at the time – ran away from the home in Monmouth and went to Ireland. First of all, we hitchhiked up north to where my friend came from.

From there, we went on the ferry to Ireland. We met some boys who gave us a place to stay and fed us with cornflakes day after day. We stayed there for about 2 months, but eventually someone told the police because there was a reward, and we were sent back to Monmouth.

Later on, I found that Thomas, my grandpa, had had a heart attack and died. I was in the home at the time and wasn't told what happened. Later on, I tried to find out where my grandma was, and tracked her down to a place on the Slade in Oxford – it used to be a barracks – a place like a hospital. I found out that my grandma had been there, but she too was dead. She used to get very excited and have full blown epileptic fits, or she'd be very anxious and that would bring on a fit for her.

Apparently, she suddenly rang the bell in the place where she was – she'd had a fit, went through the window, cutting her jugular, and died. When I found out all this, it was too late, she'd gone – I couldn't even bury her or anything. I was 17 or 18 then and of course was attached to her, so I felt this as another loss. Perhaps it affected me that no one seemed to think it important enough to tell me. It was around this time that I made my first suicide attempt. I overdosed on pills and remember waking up in hospital with Deirdre at my side.

When I was at Monmouth, I had aided and abetted some boys in stealing a car – they were also running away. They took me to where I wanted to go in Oxford, and because I wanted to prove the point that I didn't need to go back to the home, I got a job and a place to live on the Cowley Road with a couple. They didn't allow boys, which was fair enough.

I was determined to prove I could stand on my own two feet, even though when I came out of care of the local authority at around 16, I was entirely alone in the world. I had no one to help me into adulthood, very little education and no qualifications. Everything that had happened to me had left me feeling worthless and unlovable.

I got a job at the Co-op and worked there for two months. Then I did turn myself in to the police because I wanted to be discharged from care. I went to court and the judge said, "What you did was wrong, obviously, but because you've proved you can look after yourself we're going to give you six months probation". I had to go to the probation place each week so they could check me out till I was completely cleared of all that.

Life after Leaving Care

Then it started – I was looking for love and I didn't know what love was. I thought sex was love and I wanted someone to love me. I met a boy – and I got pregnant, and he left me. I didn't know what to do, and I couldn't look after the baby. I met another man, Alan, and I thought he loved me and I got pregnant again. Alan didn't want to marry me. He was an atheist, but because I had been born out of wedlock myself, I knew what that meant and it was really important to me to be married.

Alan was a very aggressive and angry kind of man, and I couldn't handle that. We were living in Fettiplace Road, and his brother was with us. Alan was angry because he didn't have cigarettes or something and so he was ready to beat me with a hammer. His brother came running in and stopped him. From then on I just didn't want to know him. Another day, the baby was crying and Alan just picked him up and threw him on the bed and he bounced off.

Then we moved to a mobile home park – Deirdre remembers us living in a caravan in a field near Farmoor Reservoir – and I realised Alan was going off with someone else. I thought: that's it. I don't want to know him anymore. So I didn't see him ever again. I knew he went off with other women, and he had children with other women and he's beat them up too. I wanted to just leave and go away because he frightened me.

I had no money, no job, and I didn't know what to do. So when somebody invited me to go to London and work as a prostitute for a while, I didn't have much choice. It was in hotels mostly, but then it was also in cars. The men picked me up in the street. I still lived in Oxford, but would go to London once a week. It was the only way I could make any money, although I didn't make much. In those days I would have charged about £50 for a hand job. A neighbour looked after the boys while I was working, but eventually, they were taken into care and put into care homes.

I due course, I was contacted and asked to give Justin, the second one, up for adoption. I met the mother and the father and found some consolation in knowing they were a Christian family so

I knew that he would be brought up wonderfully. I still see him from time to time.

He's not angry that I left him, but I've asked both of them, as grown up men, to forgive me for what I did. I thought it would be the best life for them, that's why I did it, otherwise if I could I would have kept them and looked after them and brought them up but I didn't realise, I thought it would be a good thing.

The first one, Jason, was never adopted. He grew up entirely in foster homes.

I don't get to see them much because there's nothing much to talk about, but I do have grandchildren – I've met them once or twice and that's about it.

I went to London where I was living with two gay girls in a squat. One night, I was waiting to be picked up as usual, and a man stopped in his car. But there was something about him; I was getting a bad feeling, so I let another girl go in my place. Then later, I found out that the man had murdered her. It was so nearly me. I feel so sorry for the girl as well. Another night, I was waiting to go somewhere, and missed my bus. A man stopped his car and offered me a lift. I accepted and the man said "Ok but I've got to stop off somewhere for a minute, and I agreed. What I didn't know was that there was another car behind, with three other men in it. They raped me in the car, one after another.

I didn't report it, I didn't know who to report it to. So I just went back to Oxford and sat in a chair in shock for two months. After that, I didn't want anyone to touch me, especially men. So I did it with a girl, but that wasn't my cup of tea either. Maybe it was because I just needed love, but it didn't work. The feelings wore off eventually, and I got over it. I'm not bitter today, but I still can't believe it. I know that they were Sikhs from their turbans, and because they lived in that part of London.

I remember telling this story to my optician – he was Sikh – and he said that he was so sorry. I said "It doesn't matter. I don't know why I'm telling you this, but I forgive them anyway. I don't hold no grudges".

Eventually, I went back to London and met someone who was from Pakistan who dealt with pharmaceuticals and he wanted to introduce me to someone in a textile company. I thought maybe I could earn some money by selling textiles – but instead the man employed me as a kind of maid in his house. There was no messing, nothing sexual or anything like that. I used to do things like serve teas to them and their friends. I met people who were very well off, like doctors in Harley Street. My employer then suggested I go to Pakistan to see if I could pursue the idea of selling textiles.

Going Abroad – to Pakistan and Malaysia

So I went to Lahore in Pakistan and my employers paid for a little house and a maid. I met his colleague and worked for them there. They dealt in second hand medical equipment as well as textiles. They were good people. I stayed there for a year trying to sell textiles but with little success so I gave up on that – there was no point.

I decided to go to Australia so I set off by train and got to Singapore where I met a young man, Robert. He was a jockey and I fell in love with him. Before long I was pregnant and found that I was carrying twins. Then Robert said that I could get rid of them. But I refused and said Ii couldn't do that. By this time I was living with him in Penang in Malaysia, but I couldn't give birth there because I only had visitor status, so I had to go to Hong Kong to have the babies there. Robert paid the airfare and gave me a bit of money, so I went there and had the babies, a boy and a girl, and then brought them back to Malaysia, to Penang.

I wanted to bring them up but it was difficult looking after them because Robert didn't love me, he didn't want me. He just said "I pity you because of your fate". I couldn't understand what he meant. Maybe he saw the future, but I didn't. It was around this time that I made my second suicide attempt, again with pills.

Working in Hong Kong

In the end I decided to go to Hong Kong and get a place to live. I had decided to kidnap one of my babies, Marika, but I couldn't get the little boy because he was up at the other end of the long house where we lived, with the kitchen and the lounge in between and then the toilet and the out bit. I just had to leave him. The night before, I'd had a dream that I was to take just one so I took my daughter, my only daughter, and went with her to Hong Kong. Marika is here in England today. The little boy that I left, Adrian, was brought up by Robert's sister.

I became a lady of the night, working in a Hong Kong club. I found an apartment and someone to look after Marika while

I was working. The club was called Bottoms Up. It was a topless bar.

There was a small bar, and men sat around you, and you were in the middle showing yourself, and the others were bringing drinks to you. So that was the job, every night. And sometimes there might be someone who wanted to escort you, you know, wanted to do it, so that would be 100 Hong Kong dollars – to me.

After the bar closed that was it, and I would often go off and have sex with a client. But it got to the stage where I just didn't want to work anymore. I was surviving, just surviving. The only good thing was that I was able to get a maid from the Philippines to look after Marika properly – she was only a year old when we got to Hong Kong.

After that, I worked at a place called the Volvo night Club. I worked as an escort. I would sit and talk, and drink and there were lots of men coming in together and they would choose which girl they liked. Most of them were visiting business people, not men who lived in Hong Kong. The men would send the girl of their choice a message that they wanted whatever – that might mean just going for dinner or going for full sex and that went on my wages. They were all sorts of men – some were American, some were Korean, some were Japanese, some were English.

I hated it. It was even worse when they were aggressive, and often they would be drunk. One, because he couldn't get it up, he got very aggressive and cross. I said "Sorry, forget it – here's your money. I can't help you and you can't help yourself". He'd had too much to drink. He was very angry with himself – he was young.

There was one man I met – the actor Jackie Chan – he was young then. I was his escort, but he didn't want sex. He just gave me 100 dollars when he left and said "thank you for the evening". I thought that was really kind. I hated having sex and would be grateful if I only had to do it once a night.

I was only able to motivate myself by thinking of what the money was for. Quite soon after I arrived in Hong Kong I found that I had to drink before I could do anything. I had to numb myself. I needed so much for Marika's school fees, so much for the rent, so much for the maid. There were some people who were very gracious and kind and just wanted my company, and that was a blessing to me. Some of them were quite weird – one wanted me to beat him.

I always made sure I put the condom on, and I would always go to my doctor and get checked every month, but I never got any sexually transmitted diseases at all, except from Marika's father. He must have been doing it with another woman at the same time. That freaked me out. It made me feel like an idiot. Yet I never caught anything from any of the others.

Going to the US

I can't remember how I got my birth mother's phone number, but occasionally I spoke to Kitty, who was now living in Widget, Arkansas. Once I was on the phone to her and she asked me a question. It was a Saturday or a Sunday and I was just relaxing at home, in the flat, and Kitty said to me, "how are you?" and then she said "What are you going to do when China takes back Hong Kong?" I said I didn't know. And Kitty said, "why don't you come here then?" And I said "OK, I'll come in a month".

I realised that I would have to get rid of all my possessions and hoped to sell them, but in the end I had to give most of my stuff away. But I was so happy to be leaving that it didn't matter. My mother didn't know what I was doing in Hong Kong, although I told her later, probably after I got to the US.

Before I left I wanted to talk to the other English girls that were doing the same job and I suggested we have a lunch party so that I could explain why I was leaving. We all knew each other but we never really saw each other away from work. I decided to talk to them and explain that I was going home to live with my mother in America. They said "Well that's cool" and everyone talked and felt good together. I felt that I wanted to say something more to them. I said, "some of you go out several times a night. But you've got all your life in front of you, you're still young, you can still find the right husband, have a nice family. If you need to make money, perhaps for college or this or that, studies or something, I can understand that, but I really advise you not to stay here too long."

I was in Hong Kong for 11 years, but most of my co-workers had only been there a year or so, or even less. I tried to help them and encouraged them to get away, pointing out that everyone gets old and then what can you do? The only option is to do it in the dark. I told them that I know somewhere where old sex workers work, where they earn money masturbating their clients. They don't get much for it, but that's all they can do, because they can't survive without any money. So I suggested that they wouldn't want to end up like that. I advised them to leave when they could and we all exchanged phone numbers and they promised to let me know how they were getting on. After that, the party went on and some of them gave me presents.

Marika had some lovely stamps which she had collected. I said "you can't take everything with you, you can only take one thing". So she said "I'll take these then". Me and Marika got to the airport and stayed overnight in a hotel there. Marika put her stamps under her pillow. She was so excited to get on the plane, and fly off to meet her nan that she left them behind. She was only 11. She really enjoyed her stamps and was very upset when she realised what had happened.

We arrived – and of course I hadn't seen my mum for years and I'll never forget when we got off the plane. We entered the exit corridor at the airport and we could hear someone running to us and my Kitty appeared and she gave me a huge hug. She recognised me even though she'd never seen a picture of me or anything. I don't look like my mum, who is dark, her skin was an olive colour and she had back hair. It was wonderful and when we got home to her place we just talked and talked and talked.

It was beautiful, it was really lovely actually. I think my mum regretted it all her life, all of those years, because of leaving me with grandma and grandpa.

Me and Marika met my two half-brothers and two half-sisters and their families which was lovely too, although I had met them when I was 12, but that was a long, long time ago.

Me and my mum talked about everything. I feel that Kitty knew in her heart that leaving me with my grandmother was the wrong thing to do because of her being epileptic and grandpa being a drunkard and a gambler. It was just wrong. My Auntie Pat knew that where I was living was horrible and my social worker knew it was an awful life there.

It was healing for Kitty, the relief of knowing that I wasn't angry and / or bitter towards her. I was just a bit numb, and didn't understand much at all at that time. But we talked about everything, and that first week was a wonderful week where we got really close and talked about when she was young and when I was young. Kitty didn't talk much about her boyfriend who was my dad, but she had told him she was pregnant. He went back to America, and then came back to see her in England. He said that he was engaged to be married to someone else which of course was awful. I feel that the rejection Kitty suffered contributed to her not being able to look after me and abandoning me to the miserable life I endured with my grandparents. Her new family, two girls and two boys, were all grown up and married when I went there. They seemed to accept and like me.

Born Again

It was the eldest sister, Dorelle (Dee) who asked me if I'd like to go to church. So we went to church and I thought the songs were wonderful, very uplifting! I enjoyed myself very much, I really liked it. So the week after that it was Independence Day in America and we had a lovely time in a place called Lake Afton. We met other people, and it was s day out, a really wonderful day. It was a fun time. I began to get to know them all.

The week after that there was what they called a Bring and Share, so Dee asked me again if I'd like to go, and I said I'd love to. So I went and there were lots of Christian people and they weren't bombarding me or anything like that, it was just fun, calm and comfortable. So after we'd finished the food, the pastor stood up on the picnic table and he gave the Gospel. Then he said, if anyone wants to come down, we'll baptise you in the river so Marika and I were baptised there and then.

It was a wonderful feeling because when I came out of the water ... it was very strange, it was like ... I got up, and then they prayed over me, and I walked away from there to go and dry out – it felt like luggage, things falling off me – a very bizarre feeling. It was really strange and I didn't understand what it was all about.

For two months I just cried, day and night, day and night, non-stop. I think it was a healing process, so I could start a new life. Kitty didn't mind at all, because

Dee, my oldest half-sister was born again. I'm not sure whether my mum was born again, but she believed in a Catholic way. Marika didn't want to talk about it.

Me and Marika stayed in America for a whole year – I got a job at Boeing Aircraft, and we tried to get permission to stay in the country, but at that time you had to be in a certain category to get in, which I wasn't. My mum Kitty had a green card and was married to an American but that didn't help my case.

While I was in America, I met the neighbour next door, and I feel that I wasn't really guided properly in a safe way, the Christian way. Me and the neighbour had sex. I was on the Pill at that time, and thought I would be safe. I started feeling strange, like I had a virus or something. So I went to the doctor's and they checked me, and told me I was pregnant. The neighbour was a single man, and he'd had a few drinks. So my mum said to me, "You can't live here and have this baby" and he paid for me to have an abortion. I felt that my mum could have been more supportive to my wish to have the child.

Kitty's husband was an aggressive kind of man because he was an alcoholic. He worked as a specialist lab technician, testing blood, and he would have a lot of drink at night. One night, Kitty said to her husband, "You'd better get some chewing gum because you smell of alcohol" and he grabbed her by the neck and made a mark all round her neck – he nearly killed her, just because she had said that. I didn't even know this until she picked me up to go to work (we were both working in the same place). She was in shock, she looked in a right state, and I said, "What's wrong, mum?"And she said, "He tried to strangle me because I told him his breath smells of alcohol". It was awful. She put up with a lot.

She passed away a long while ago, she had problems with her heart and she had a triple bypass, and she was also diabetic, so that didn't really help at all. Because she had a job, all the medical help was there – she knew she was going to die and her daughters were each side of her, holding her hands. I got a phone call to say that all of a sudden she let go their hands and put her hands up and she died. I believe that God was calling her home and that an angel takes you home, and that I will see her again – and my grandmother too.

Going Back to Oxford

Eventually, me and Marika had to go back to England, although we'd have rather stayed in the US. When we got back to Oxford, I went to the police and asked them to help because we were homeless. We came to Oxford because it was the only place I knew. I was very depressed because I'd come back to a life I had hated. The police sent us to the Housing Office, and we were put into a kind of bed and breakfast on the Cowley Road, near the Regal cinema. We were there for about 8 months. It wasn't too bad, at least it was near where I used to live, although my grandparents were dead by then. Marika went to school – she went in America a bit and of course she had been to school in Hong Kong for a while. Later on, they went from Cowley

Road to Cutteslowe. Deirdre remembers being in contact with me again at the Homeless Families Unit there, the first time she had seen me since the time I was with Alan. There were some little flats there. They had one bedroom and a bed you could bring down, so I would sleep on that in the lounge, and Marika would sleep in the bedroom. Then we went to Wolvercote and Marika went to yet another school – Cherwell.

By this time, I had started attending Oxford bible Church. I remember at some point going to the pastors' Derek and Hilary's house group, and there was a woman there who talked about abortions. She told me that her husband had demanded that she get rid of her baby, and because she was married she thought she had to obey her husband, so she had an abortion. This story made me realise that I hadn't forgiven myself for having my abortion. The woman suggested to me that I give a name to the child I aborted. I thought, Wow! I never realised that I could give my child a name, and I was surprised. When I went home, I was in my bedroom, and I asked God, I said, "Please forgive me". I lost one baby in Malaysia a long time ago, and of course this one I aborted. I said "Lord, I want to give these children names." So I named them Jacob and Elijah.

When I said those names, I heard an audible voice saying "Children, your mother is giving you names". I've never forgotten that. I know I will meet them – they are already there.

My New Life

It was at the Oxford Bible Church that I met the man who became my husband, Terry. I didn't know him at all. He was just a young Christian. There was a guest speaker in church who had come from America. He talked about healing from the Bible. After he finished his sermon, he came up and said to me "do you know this man?" I said No. He said "this is Terry, my brother in Christ, that's all I know". And he put our hands together and said, "God has a plan for you both". I thought, "What can that be?" And here we are, still married many decades later.

I feel that, until then, I didn't know what love is. I thought sex was love, I really did. And because I thought sex was love,

I got pregnant three times and had four children. But I could not understand, and could not look after them because I was still a child myself. There was no help in those days, many decades ago.

Later, I worked at St Edward's School, a boarding school in the Woodstock Road, Oxford. I also wanted to make things right with God, and have another child. Me and Terry tried for two years to have a baby and it just wasn't working. I wasn't having periods at all, but if Sarah in the Old Testament could have a child as an older woman, why couldn't I? I really believed this, so I asked the church to believe in me, and one night, when I tried to conceive, it was very different. It was a very bizarre feeling, it was like a boom. I still remember the feeling, and soon afterwards my pregnancy was confirmed. When I went into labour, the monitor was showing the baby getting stressed, so they had to get him out really quickly. He didn't even cry, he was such a precious child.

After he was born I carried on working at St Edwards for a while. I would bring Luke to work and lay him on the bed when I went to another part of the school. Then I worked for a family of three children and a husband and wife, and they had their own house at the school and I was able to bring him to work. Then he started to get a bit older, and I was worried he might fall down the stairs or something. So I had to give up in the end, when he was about 2 and a half. Terry was working as a postman.

When my son was about 5 and went to school, I was able to work at the John Radcliffe hospital.

Marika stayed on at school. She wanted to leave home at 18 to go and do her own thing. She did some course at college, but then she got a problem with her back. She has a daughter.

When I had come back to Oxford and was so down, I didn't get tempted to go back on the game. I'd got past all that. I thought "no, no". And then when I met Terry, of course things completely changed and I wanted to put things right. I wanted to change my lifestyle, I really did. It was the most important thing in my life. At last, I had broken the mould and been able to make a relationship with a man who was not like all the other men in my life (and my mother's life) who had been violent, alcoholic, unfaithful, unloving, unsupportive or had deserted me – my birth father, my grandfather, the fathers of my first four children.

I felt that God took me out of the pit, from something awful to something wonderful. I'm just glad that I knew my birth mother. I never met my biological father, I only know his name. I would like a picture. I must look like him because I don't look anything like my mother.

I worked there for 5 years. I loved caring for the people, especially the elderly patients. I would share the Gospel with them. There was one man who called out to me for help so I went to him and found that he'd soiled himself. I cleaned him up and made him comfortable. I had the thought that I should share the Gospel with him so I asked him if he wanted to ask Jesus into his heart and he said yes. I explained what Jesus did for him and helped him pray the prayer of salvation. Then it was time for dinner, so I stayed with him for that. Afterwards, I was about to go but he begged me to stay with him, so I held both his hands and said I would stay with him. He was still holding my hands when his head flopped to the side and I thought he had fainted so I went and got a doctor. But the doctor told me he had died. I was so surprised because it was so sudden, almost as soon as he had given his heart to the Lord.

Eventually I had to stop working in the hospital. Some people didn't like me because I was so open with my faith to patients. There was a man who was fitting, and I held him, but people said I was praying with him and they made it so that I had to leave.

Now I'm retired. I go to town most days and share the Gospel with people that I meet on the bus or in the street. I hand out tracts and share the love of the Lord. It's not about me, it's about my Father. It's the love of my Father that I was searching for all my life and I found it, so now I share it with anyone I meet.

Appendices

1: My Reasons for Writing This

One of the reasons I want to share my story is to show young people, especially those who might be drawn into sex work, that there are other pathways. I want to encourage youngsters to make use of any support these is, but especially my church. Contact details are below.

My story also challenges the myth that most sex workers have made a positive career choice. Perhaps a few do, but my story shows rather how young people who grow up without love and stability can be more likely to drift into prostitution. Perhaps prostitution reinforces the low self-esteem we often experience, making us feel even more worthless. It is estimated that about 70% of sex workers have grown up in care. As this can mean lots of changes and a disrupted education, looked-after children often have fewer qualifications and therefore fewer career choices. This makes the financial rewards of various kinds of sex work even more tempting. So the cycle goes on, but as we have seen with my story, the cycle can be broken.

2: What is love? The Answer to my Question

Love is patient and kind; love does not envy or boast; it is not arrogant or rude. It does not insist on its own way; it is not irritable or resentful; it does not rejoice in wrongdoing, but rejoices with the truth. Love bears all things, believes all things, hopes all things, endures all things. Love never ends.

1 Corinthians 13

Oh Lord you have searched me and known me! How precious to me are your thoughts oh God! How vast is the sum of them! If I would count them, they are more than the sand. Search me oh God, and know my heart! Try me and know my thoughts! Even before a word is on my tongue, behold O Lord, you know it altogether.

Psalm 139 verses 1, 18 and 23

There is no fear in love, but perfect love casts out fear. For fear has to do with punishment, and whoever fears has not been perfected in love

1 John 4 verse 18

We love because He first loved us.
1 John 4 verse 19

For God so loved the world, that He gave His only Son, that whoever believes in Him should not perish but have eternal life

John 3 verse 16

3: What Now?

God's Amazing Love

I have shared with you my story to give you a glimpse of God's amazing love, which has transformed my heart and my life. Without His love, I would be a lost soul. But He reached down to me and saved me and filled my heart with His love. He proved His love for me by dying on the Cross for my sins and rising again to give me new life. He pursued me with his love, even when I was in the darkness, and He rescued me, and I am so grateful to Him

If He did this for me, then He will do the same for you, whatever situation you are in. Just know that He loves you, turn to Him and ask Him into your heart and life to save you and make you a new creation.

The Bible promises that all who call upon the Name of the Lord Jesus shall be saved (Romans 10 verse 13).

You can do this by saying this prayer from your heart.

Prayer

Dear God in heaven, thank you for loving me. Thank you for sending Jesus, your Son, to die for me and save me from my sin and give me Eternal Life with you.

Right now, Jesus, I ask you to come into my heart and be my Saviour and Lord. Please forgive all my sin and fill my heart with Your Love.

I put my trust in you and give my life to you. I confess that Jesus is my Lord. Thank you for saving me. Amen.

**FOR MORE INFORMATION,
please contact:**

Oxford Bible Church

Pastors Derek and Hilary Walker.

Phone: 01865 515-086

Email: <u>obc.church@yahoo.co.uk</u>

Website: www.oxfordbiblechurch.co.uk

Printed in Dunstable, United Kingdom